**MIRIAM MOSS** was born in England and has lived in the Middle East, Africa and China. She taught English in the UK and Kenya before beginning her writing career. She is an award-winning author of 75 books, translated into 21 languages. Her books for Frances Lincoln include *Arctic Song*, *Jungle Song*, *This is the Oasis* and *This is the Tree*, all illustrated by Adrienne Kennaway. Miriam lives in Sussex with her family.

**ADRIENNE KENNAWAY** was born in New Zealand and grew up in Kenya where she spent many years. She studied at Ealing Art School and the Accademia di Belle Arti in Rome. She loves painting animals, and learned how to scuba dive in order to paint tropical marine fish. Adrienne won the Kate Greenaway Medal for her book *Crafty Chameleon*. Her previous books for Frances Lincoln are *Curious Clownfish* and *Rainbow Bird* by Eric Maddern, and *Arctic Song*, *Jungle Song*, *This is the Tree* and *This is the Oasis*, which are all written by Miriam Moss. Adrienne lives in County Kerry, in Ireland.

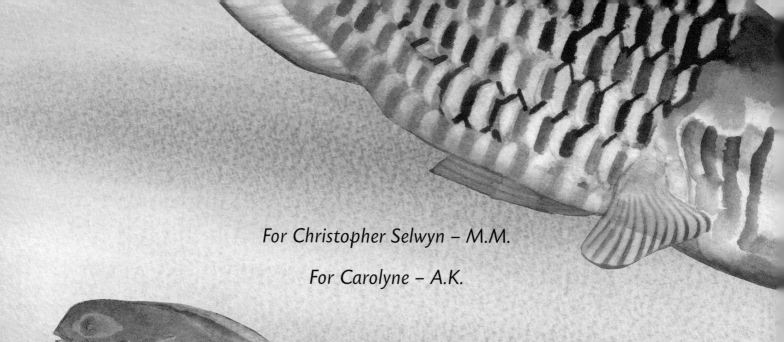

*For Christopher Selwyn – M.M.*

*For Carolyne – A.K.*

**The Publishers would like to thank Dr Paul Marshall from the
Great Barrier Reef Marine Park Authority and Professor Geoff Jones
from James Cook University for acting as consultants on this book.**

*This is the Reef* copyright © Frances Lincoln Limited 2007
Text copyright © Miriam Moss 2007
Illustrations copyright © Adrienne Kennaway 2007

First published in Great Britain and in the USA in 2007 by Frances Lincoln Children's Books,
4 Torriano Mews, Torriano Avenue, London NW5 2RZ

www.franceslincoln.com

First paperback edition published 2008

British Library Cataloguing in Publication Data available on request

ISBN 978-1-84507-659-7

The illustrations for this book are in watercolour

Printed in Singapore

1 3 5 7 9 8 6 4 2

# This is the Reef

# Reef

Miriam Moss

Illustrated by
Adrienne Kennaway

**F**

FRANCES LINCOLN
CHILDREN'S BOOKS

This is the place bathed in warm azure water,
fringed with white breakers
under tropical skies.

This is the place full of wonderful wildlife,
so vast and astonishing
you can see it from space!

This is the place made of countless small creatures,
a bright city of coral,
slow-built over time.

This is the place of fantastic formations –
of tubes, trees and antlers,
brains, feathers and fans.

This is the place where carnivals of fish drift
through clear coral gardens
in soft swaying seas.

This is the place where a lionfish yawns
at a black-spotted snapper
with wide worried eyes.

This is the place where fish-eating flowers
waft poison-tipped tentacles
to paralyse prey.

This is the place where a huge shoal of silversides
shift, spiral, then shiver
with the shock of attack.

This is the place where fish crowd for cleaning
by busy striped wrasses,
while a turtle flips by.

This is the place where a manta ray glides
with a halo of striped jacks
and slow-flexing wings.

This is the place where lobsters go trundling,
and a hermit crab scuttles,
wide eyes out on stalks.

This is the place where slow-moving nudibrachs
advertise nastiness
in bright coloured stripes.

This is the place where an army of parrot fish
chomp chunks of coral
while searching for food.

This is the place where the crown of thorns starfish,
deadly killer of coral,
devours the reef.

This is the place, when sunlight starts fading,
where fish hide in crevices
for fear of attack.

This is the place where sharks squeeze and slither,
sense movements in water
and stab at trapped fish.

This is the place where a moray eel in moonlight
snakes over the seabed
while searching for prey.

This is the place where cloud-bursts of coral eggs
drift off on a warm tide
into wide, open seas.

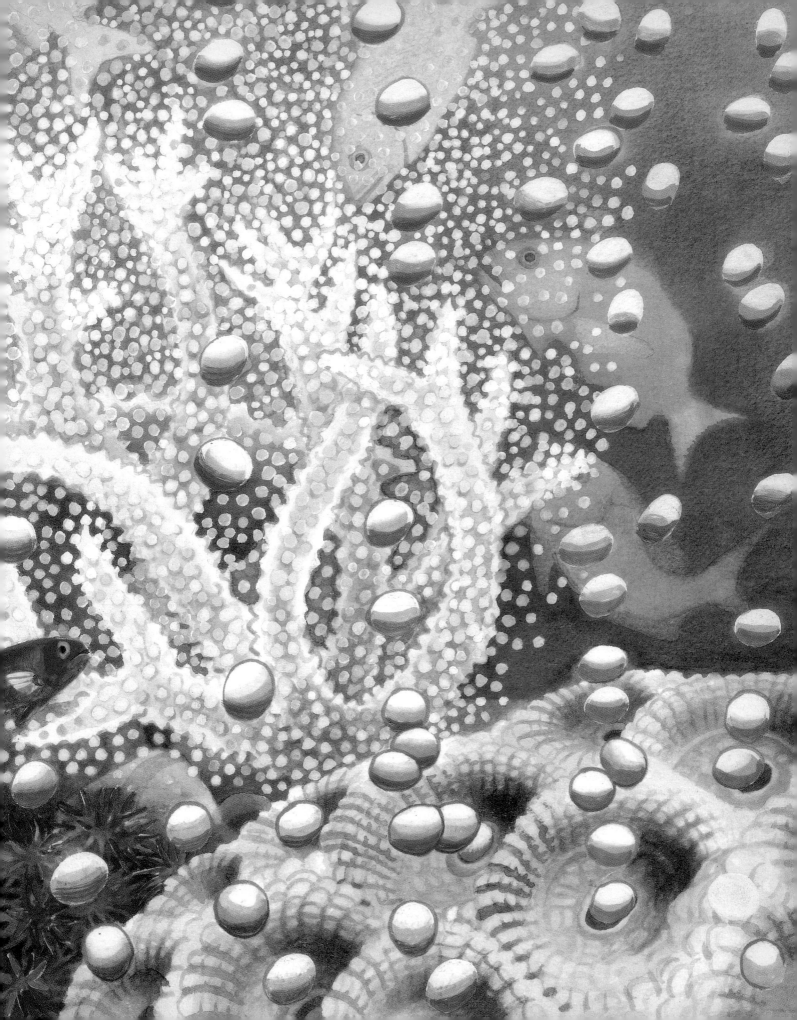

This is the place, when the wind builds a cyclone,
where creatures sense danger
while stormy seas swell.

This is the place where waves high as mountains
crash down with such fury,
they smash up the reef.

This is the place where a lone humpback calls
singing strong, haunting songs
in his search for a mate.

This is the place bathed in warm azure water
and fringed with white breakers
under tropical skies.

This is the Great Barrier Reef.

# Also appearing in this book

Paddletail

Scissortail Sergeant

Lined Butterflyfish

Orange Seastar

Anthias

Half and Half Chromis

Widestripe Fusilier

Midas Blenny

Threadfin Butterflyfish

Ambone Toby

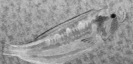

Surge Wrasse

Elongate Surgeonfish

Coral Hind

Golden Trevally

Square Spot Anthias

Regal Angelfish

Orange-striped Triggerfish

Red Soldierfish

Copperbanded Butterflyfish

Chisseltooth Wrasse

Pinnate Batfish

Lemon Damsel

## Coral

Coral reefs are made from millions of tiny creatures called coral polyps that live in colonies. The polyps have soft bodies surrounded by hard skeletons. When they die their tiny skeletons are left behind. The coral reef forms gradually as new polyps grow over the old ones. Many of the Earth's reefs are thousands of years old.

## Endangered Reefs

These delicate, ancient reefs are easily destroyed by dramatic natural events such as hurricanes, but the main threat to coral reefs comes from humans. Trampling feet, the anchors of boats and the fins of divers easily destroy the fragile coral. Reefs are damaged when people collect coral, shells and other creatures to sell as souvenirs, or when they catch fish by using explosives to stun them. In parts of the world coral reefs are also destroyed when they are used to build roads and houses.

Pollution poisons coral, and sewage and fertilizers running into the sea increase the growth of algae and seaweeds which then suffocate the reef. Coral is also sensitive to the smallest change in temperature, so global warming is a real threat. If the waters around coral becomes too warm the coral turns white. This is called *bleaching*.

Many people are trying to save coral reefs by creating marine parks that protect the living coral and encourage people to care for the reefs. The biggest marine park in the world is the Great Barrier Reef Marine Park off the north-east coast of Australia. It covers 345,000 square kilometres (138,000 square miles).

# MORE BOOKS BY MIRIAM MOSS AND ADRIENNE KENNAWAY
# FROM FRANCES LINCOLN CHILDREN'S BOOKS

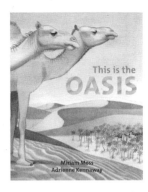

### This is the Oasis

Have you ever wondered how anything survives in a
hot desert climate?
This is the celebration of an oasis – a green jewel in the Sahara –
and its importance for the plant, animal and human life
that surrounds it. With facts about the Sahara and the Tuareg
people, this is a perfect introduction to the harsh but beautiful
desert wilderness and the life that it supports.

### This is the Tree

The ancient and extraordinary baobab tree takes centre stage
in this poetic and informative story of the wildlife of Africa.
Old as a volcano, the distinctive 'upside-down' tree plays a vital
role in the lives of numerous creatures. Buffalo doze beneath it,
the bushbaby burgles its flowers, elephants feed on it,
and the turaco bird nests among its branches.

### Jungle Song

When Little Tapir is woken by Spider and led deep into the
jungle, he meets all sorts of wildlife, who add their own rhythms
to the wild song. But when the beat stops and Little Tapir is all
alone, he realises just how dangerous the jungle song can be!

Frances Lincoln titles are available from all good bookshops.
You can also buy books and find out more about your favourite titles,
authors and illustrators on our website: www.franceslincoln.com